Aldo Leopold

Aldo LEOPOLD
Protector of the Wild

Della Yannuzzi

Gateway Green
The Millbrook Press
Brookfield, Connecticut

This book is dedicated to my great-niece, Katlyn Ann Ross.

Cover photographs courtesy of the Aldo Leopold Foundation (© Charles C. Bradley) and Visuals Unlimited, Inc. (© Fritz Polking)

Photographs courtesy of the Aldo Leopold Foundation Archives: pp. 6, 19, 27, 32, 33, 37 (© Charles C. Bradley), 39 (© Thomas C. Coleman); Photo Researchers, Inc.: pp. 9 (© Maslowski), 44 (© Leonard Lee Rue III); Visuals Unlimited, Inc.: pp. 10 (© Fritz Polking), 22 (© Chick Piper); The Lawrenceville School/Bunn Library: p. 13; University of Wisconsin/Madison Archives: pp. 14, 29, 35; Yale University Library: pp. 16, 17; North Wind Picture Archives: p. 24; New Mexico Department of Tourism: p. 25; © David Muench 2001: p. 43

Library of Congress Cataloging-in-Publication Data
Yannuzzi, Della A.
Aldo Leopold : protector of the wild / Della A. Yannuzzi.
p. cm. — (Gateway green)
Includes bibliographical references.
Summary: A biography of the American naturalist who was a leader in wildlife conservation.
ISBN 0-7613-2465-8 (lib. bdg.)
1. Leopold, Aldo, 1887–1948—Juvenile literature. 2. Naturalists—Wisconsin—Biography—Juvenile literature. [1. Leopold, Aldo, 1887–1948. 2. Naturalists.] I. Title. II. Gateway green biography.
QH31.L618 Y36 2002 333.7'2'092—dc21 [B] 2001044425

Published by The Millbrook Press
2 Old New Milford Road
Brookfield, Connecticut 06804
www.millbrookpress.com

Aldo Leopold

Aldo Leopold

From an early age, Aldo Leopold enjoyed exploring the fields and woods surrounding his home in Burlington, Iowa. Aldo loved the outdoors so much that sometimes he skipped school. He and his dog, a cocker spaniel named Spud, wandered along the cliffs beneath his home or headed to the banks of the Mississippi River to watch the migrating birds.

Aldo's father also loved the outdoors. Aldo and his brothers and sister would often go with their father on field trips into the woods to learn about wildlife. Aldo grew up loving and respecting nature. He would always try to protect the wild places and wildlife. This is his story.

Growing Up

Rand Aldo Leopold was born on January 11, 1887, in Burlington, Iowa. His first name was quickly dropped in favor of Aldo. He and his family lived in his grandparents' large house, which sat on a cliff overlooking the Mississippi River.

When Aldo was a young child, his grandfather built a house for Aldo's family on land behind his own home. He also built a walking trail along the cliffs, so his grandchildren had a good view of the Mississippi River and the passing riverboats. Wetlands and prairies surrounded the town of Burlington. These wilderness areas attracted many kinds of birds and animals.

Aldo had many chances to enjoy nature because both his father and grandfather had outdoor hobbies. Aldo's father, Carl, was a traveling salesman and later became part owner of a furniture company. In his spare time, he often took Aldo on long hikes into the woods. He showed him the habits of animals, such as where they slept and what they fed on.

Aldo's father was also a hunter, but he respected wildlife. He had his own hunting rules since there were not many laws to protect birds, ducks, and small game. He never hunted in the spring, when the number of birds was low, and he never hunted rare animals.

When he was young, Aldo kept records
of wrens and other birds that were in
his backyard.

Yellowstone National Park was Aldo's favorite vacation spot as a teenager. The park is mostly in Wyoming, but parts of it also lie in Montana and Idaho.

Aldo's grandfather was a successful businessman and architect and loved the outdoors. He enjoyed birding and gardening. He taught Aldo the names of many birds and plants.

One summer, Aldo kept a written record of more than one hundred baby wrens that hatched in his backyard. By the time he was eleven years old, he had identified and listed the names of thirty-nine bird species in his notebook. Aldo's habit of watching nature became a way of life for him.

When Aldo was a teenager, the Leopold family began to spend summers on Marquette Island in Michigan. There were many open and wild places to explore. Aldo would often disappear into the woods, where he hiked, watched the wildlife, and hunted small game. He also sailed and fished on Lake Huron and often cooked the fish on an open fire.

At the age of sixteen, Aldo went with his family on a vacation to Yellowstone National Park. He could not believe the natural wonders that surrounded him—so open, free, and wild. He later wrote in his journal: "There is no better possible vacation."

Leaving Home

When Aldo was in his junior year at Burlington High School, he had a decision to make. His mother suggested he go to the Lawrenceville Preparatory School in New Jersey. Aldo's father thought he should stay at Burlington High School and then go to Iowa State University. After graduation, he could then enter the family furniture business.

But Aldo did not want to sell furniture. He decided the New Jersey school would give him a better chance of getting into a new forestry program at Yale University. Aldo's parents supported his choice even though they would miss him. Aldo was uncertain about this big change, but he was also excited.

Aldo arrived at school in January, and had to catch up with the other students. He worked hard to get good grades. His heavy class schedule of English, German, algebra, geometry, and other subjects kept him busy. Aldo was a serious person, but he also liked to have fun. He joined the baseball team and swam in the school's pool.

Before long the outdoors called to him. Aldo was soon taking long walks through the woods, fields, farmland, and marshes around the school. He always carried binoculars, a notebook, and a pen. He even named the areas he explored. There were Cat Woods, Big Woods, Owl Woods, and others.

Lawrenceville Preparatory School

Aldo while attending Lawrenceville

In time, he invited some of his new school friends on outdoor hikes. He liked to call this "tramping." They roamed the area to watch the migrating birds. Sometimes they climbed up big oak trees for a better view. Unfortunately, Aldo stayed outdoors so much that he began to skip classes. Some of his grades dropped. The school had to help Aldo set time aside for his studies.

While he was at Lawrenceville, Aldo sent letters home. He wrote about his grades, his teachers, the people he met, and his nature discoveries. In one letter he wrote: "Flickers and blue jays are beginning to increase in number as the weather grows warmer. Song sparrows and meadowlarks are singing constantly, while robins and fox sparrows are just beginning to try a few notes."

Forest School and Work

In the spring of 1905, when Aldo graduated from Lawrenceville, he knew he wanted an outdoors career. He was ready to continue his studies at Yale's Forest School.

Aldo during his Yale years

The Yale program was the first in the country to offer courses in forestry. It included fieldwork at a summer camp in Pennsylvania. Here, Aldo learned how to take care of the forests.

Aldo graduated from the Yale Forest School in February 1909. He was one of thirty-five men to graduate that year from the country's first forestry program. In early March, he spent more than two months at another forest

Yale Forest School in the early 1900s

camp in Texas. He passed a Civil Service test. Now he could work for the United States Forest Service.

When Aldo was twenty-two years old, he began work as a forest assistant. He was assigned to the Apache National Forest in Arizona Territory. He looked like a cowboy in his forest ranger clothes, long leather boots, and wide-brimmed hat.

Aldo rode his horse, Jiminy Hicks, through the forest. He was given a pair of guns to frighten away bears, mountain lions, and bobcats. Aldo's dog, Flick, joined him on his trips into the woods.

Aldo's job kept him busy. He inspected trees and marked the diseased ones that needed to be cut. This prevented the diseases from spreading to the healthy trees. He also kept track of grazing and hunting permits, water rights, and the number of trees cut down by lumber companies.

Many cattle and sheep ranchers obeyed grazing laws, but some did not. One of Aldo's most important jobs was to protect the forestlands from overgrazing. When too many animals always fed in the same place, the overgrazing exposed the soil. When there were heavy rains, the soil washed away because there wasn't enough grass to hold it in place. This resulted in less food for the wildlife.

Sometimes lumber companies cut down too many trees. Aldo had to enforce timber laws. He made sure that only the legal number of trees was cut. Companies paid fines when they did not obey the laws.

Aldo performed so well that he was promoted to Forest Deputy Supervisor of the Carson National Forest in New Mexico. Here, he met a pretty teacher named Estella Bergere. He fell in love with her and proposed marriage. Estella accepted his proposal. They were married on October 9, 1912, and moved into a house in the woods. Aldo and Estella called their new home *Mia Casita*—"My Little House."

In the spring of 1913, Aldo had to leave *Mia Casita* to take care of some problems in another forest district. Farmers were protesting against some of the

Aldo with his new bride, Estella Bergere Leopold

Forest Service's rules. Aldo took a train and then rode into the district on horseback. He cleared up the disagreement, and then he was eager to get back to Estella. She was going to have a baby.

The weather turned cold and rainy as he headed home on his horse. Aldo shivered underneath his wet clothes. He decided to take a shortcut but got lost in the woods. When he finally found the right road, his legs were so swollen that he could hardly walk.

He made his way to a doctor in a nearby town. The doctor said he had rheumatism, a sickness that makes the joints and muscles stiff and sore. Aldo made it home, but his arms and legs were so swollen that he could barely move.

His fellow rangers sent him to another doctor. The new doctor told him he had nephritis, a kidney disease that causes swelling. Aldo almost died. He had to stop working and stay in bed for almost two months. It took him more than a year to fully recover.

Aldo spent this time with his wife and their first child, Aldo Starker Leopold, who was born on October 22, 1913. Although Aldo missed working outdoors, he kept busy reading nature books. He also wrote articles for the *Pine Cone*, the Carson Forest newsletter. He thought a lot about his future and how he could continue to protect the wild places and their wildlife.

21

Protecting the Wild Places

Because of his illness, Aldo was offered an office job at forest headquarters in Albuquerque, New Mexico. It wasn't an outdoor job, but he was happy to be working again.

Soon Aldo was researching wildlife management. He learned that wildlife such as wild turkey, antelope, and mountain sheep needed protection or they would become extinct. He began writing a guidebook for forest rangers in the southwestern region of the United States. The book outlined a plan to protect and increase game animals in the forests.

On December 22, 1914, Aldo's father died. Aldo became even more determined to do something for the wilderness that his father loved so much. But Aldo felt that nobody in the forest service was listening to his ideas. He was wrong. Arthur Ringland, his boss and the district chief, paid attention. He offered Aldo a new job teaching people how to care for the beautiful lands in and around the Grand Canyon in Arizona.

Aldo studied the history of the Grand Canyon, its rivers and its woods. He traveled around the forest areas, and he grew very concerned. People were not taking care of the land or its wildlife. Trash littered campsites. Fish were scarce in the rivers, and hunters killed game out of season.

Too many roads were being built. Run-down shacks and cabins dotted the landscape. He worried that beautiful wild

Aldo became very concerned about the condition of the Grand Canyon when he realized that people were not taking care of the land.

places would disappear if people didn't care more about the natural world. They had to learn to respect the land in order to take care of it.

Aldo began to speak to nature clubs and citizen groups interested in the environment. He became secretary of the Albuquerque branch of the New Mexico Game Protective Association. Theodore Roosevelt, who had set aside more than 150 million acres (60 million hectares) of land as wildlife protected areas, wrote Aldo a letter. He praised Aldo's work in protecting the nation's wild places.

Slowly, people began to listen to Aldo's ideas about respecting and caring for the land. They formed citizen organizations and looked for ways to help protect wildlife.

In the fall of 1916, when Aldo was almost thirty years old, his kidney problems returned. He had to take time off from his job to rest, but there was still more work to do. He decided to leave the Forest Service and to find a job that put him before the public.

He went to work for the City of Albuquerque in New Mexico. He was to interest people in taking care of their city parks and the Rio Grande river. He stayed in this job for about a year.

Then the Forest Service offered him an important job. He accepted and became an assistant forester in charge of opera-

President Theodore Roosevelt greatly approved of the work that Aldo was doing to protect wildlife.

tions in the Southwest. Aldo had to inspect and report on all the forests in the surrounding area. He observed soil erosion, when soil is lost or carried off by wind, water, or overgrazing. During this time, he wrote another book, called the *Watershed Handbook.* It was the first Forest Service manual on soil erosion control.

Aldo did not like what he found during his forest inspections. Heavy sheep-grazing was stripping the land of its grasses and plants. This overgrazing caused soil loss during heavy rains. Aldo wanted to save land in the Gila National Forest around the head of the Gila River. He wrote a report outlining his ideas and gave it to the Chief Forester.

Aldo's report stated that no more grazing permits should be issued and no more homes and businesses built in the area. Aldo's plan for the Gila Wilderness Area was approved. This

The Gila Wilderness Area became the first officially protected wilderness region in a national forest.

became the first protected official wilderness region in a national forest. Soon, other wildlife areas were set aside. People began calling Aldo the "Father of the National Wilderness System."

Writing and Teaching

In 1924, Aldo, his wife, and their four children left New Mexico and moved to Madison, Wisconsin. Aldo had a new job with the Forest Service. He was named assistant director of the Forest Products Laboratory. The laboratory conducted tests on wood to improve many wood products.

Although he did a good job, Aldo was not interested in office work. He missed the outdoors and his work with wildlife. After three years, he began to look for another job. He left the Forest Service again and worked for different nature groups and local businesses.

In 1928, Aldo finally had a chance to work on a wildlife survey for The Sporting Arms and Ammunition Manufact-

This portrait of Aldo was taken when he began his wildlife survey in 1928.

urers' Institute. This survey aimed to develop ideas to conserve game animals.

Aldo traveled around the country and studied different wildlife. He talked to farmers, birders, and ecologists—scientists who study soil, plants, animals, and their habitats. He took notes and drew charts and maps. He read many books on ecology.

Aldo learned that in some areas the numbers of wild turkey and pheasant were decreasing because their natural homes were not protected. Grassy places, woods, ponds, and brush where wildlife nested and found food were disappearing.

In 1931, Aldo's wildlife survey report was published. He stated that people needed to learn how to conserve natural resources. Aldo wanted his children, now five in number, and all the children of the world to enjoy the wilderness. He taught his children to respect the land and its wildlife. When they grew up, they each worked in nature- and science-related jobs.

In 1933, the University of Wisconsin offered Aldo a job teaching the country's first advanced program in game management. In the beginning, Aldo's office was located in two small rooms in the basement of the University Soils Building. Then the university let him use an old house. This gave him enough room for a big office, a library, a laboratory, and a place for student discussions.

Aldo working in his classroom at the University of Wisconsin

Aldo was a popular teacher, called "The Professor" by his students. He took them on field trips and asked them to look for animal prints and changes in the soil.

The next year, Aldo was offered another job in addition to teaching. President Franklin Roosevelt had set aside money for wildlife refuge grounds. He appointed Aldo and two other people to serve on the President's Committee on Wildlife Restoration. This committee was formed to protect the nation's wildlife.

"The Shack"

In his personal life, Aldo always tried to take care of the land. He and his family lived according to this belief. In 1935, Aldo bought a rundown farm with a shabby chicken house on the Wisconsin River. He planned to restore the land and the chicken house with the help of his family.

The Leopold family called their new vacation home "The Shack." They raised the roof on the chicken house, cleaned up the inside, and added a fireplace. Aldo and his children planted prairie grasses and thousands of white and red pine trees. Aldo's wife planted wildflowers.

They recycled fallen trees by using the wood to make shelves and a table for the house. In their spare time, they enjoyed the land and its many birds and other wildlife. Aldo loved to get up early in the morning and write in his nature journal at an outdoor table. One day he wrote in his journal: "The skunk track leads on, showing no interest in possible food, and no concern over the rompings or retributions of his neighbors. I wonder what he has on his mind; what got him out of bed?"

Aldo did a lot of thinking at his nature home. He was developing a concept that he called the "Land Ethic." He pointed out that the land is made up of animals, plants, and soils, and

The Leopold farm in the 1930s

if one is upset or hurt, the others will feel it. He believed conservation was based on the harmony between people and the land.

One time, Aldo saw a wolf get shot. He looked into the wolf's eyes before it died and later said he had seen "a fierce green fire in his eyes." Aldo never forgot that look of defiance in the wolf's eyes.

Aldo had always thought predators such as wolves, bear, and mountain lions threatened the numbers of wild game. He came to understand that there had to be a balance in nature. Predators like the wolf helped control the number of deer and other wildlife in the forest.

Aldo planned to publish his journal notes as a book. He called this collection *Great Possessions*. He sent the manuscript to a publisher, but it was rejected. Aldo continued to work on it.

Aldo enjoyed writing and doing research outside surrounded by the wilderness.

Aldo Leopold's Legacy

While he was busy with all this work, Aldo became ill. He began to get terrible pains in his face. The doctors said his facial nerves were swollen and inflamed, and that he might need surgery.

Aldo decided to rest at The Shack. He was now almost sixty years old and had spent a lifetime trying to protect the wild places. Aldo hoped he had changed the way people thought about the great outdoors. He hoped they would take care of the natural world.

In late summer 1947, Aldo's face pains grew worse. He had to have surgery. This operation left his face numb and sagging. He had trouble speaking, and his words came out mumbled and slurred. Not long after this, Aldo's eyes began to bother him. He had eye surgery and then wore an eye patch.

Little by little, Aldo's eyes healed, and his speech and strength began to return. He continued to teach his classes and asked his son Luna to find a publisher for his book. He was pleased when the U. S. government asked him to represent the country at a conference on conservation. Then on April 14, 1948, more good news arrived. Oxford University Press offered to publish his book.

On Friday, April 16, 1948, Aldo, his wife, and his daughter Estella and her boyfriend drove to The Shack for a restful

Aldo absorbed in his work soon before he became ill

weekend. On Sunday, Estella's boyfriend went home, but Aldo and his family stayed at the farm. They planted more trees, walked around their land, and did other chores.

On Wednesday, April 21, the Leopold family saw smoke rising near a neighbor's farm. As Aldo watched, the smoke began to blow toward their own farm. Aldo and his family gathered up shovels, gloves, water cans, buckets, and a fire pump and drove to the neighbor's farm.

A brushfire was spreading to the pine trees on Aldo's land. People were trying to put it out. Aldo strapped the fire pump onto his back and sent his daughter to call the local fire department. Then he moved into the brush and sprayed the burning grass. While fighting the fire, Aldo Leopold had a heart attack and died. The firemen found him on the ground, his arms folded on his chest. He was sixty-one years old.

After his death, Aldo's book of nature essays was published. It was now called *A Sand County Almanac*. He wrote in his book: "Wilderness is a resource which can shrink but not grow."

His writing shows the beauty of nature and its wildlife. One piece is called "If I Were the Wind." It begins: "The wind that makes music in November corn is in a hurry. The stalks hum, the loose husks whisk skyward in half-playful swirls, and the wind hurries on." It concludes: "It is warm behind the drift-

The Leopold farm in recent years

wood now, for the wind has gone with the geese. So would I—if I were the wind."

After Aldo's death, the Leopold family decided to protect The Shack and the family land by creating the Aldo Leopold Foundation. This organization helps people understand the ideas of conservation and care of the wilderness.

The pine trees that Aldo and his family planted are still on the property. The colorful fields of wildflowers and prairie grasses still grow there. Wildlife scurries through the woods, and birds rest in the trees and on the ground, free and protected, as Aldo had wanted.

Today there are nearly 105 million acres (42 million hectares) of federally protected wilderness. His ideas have spread all over the United States. Millions of Americans visit and enjoy the natural, wild places that Aldo Leopold spent his life trying to protect and save.

**Aldo will always be remembered as the
"Father of the National Wilderness System."**

CHRONOLOGY

1887	Born Rand Aldo Leopold on January 11 in Burlington, Iowa.
1904	Attends Lawrenceville Preparatory School in New Jersey.
1905–1907	Enrolls at Yale's Sheffield Scientific School, then moves on to Yale University's Forest School.
1909	Graduates from Yale Forest School and begins work with the U.S. Forest Service.
1912	Marries Estella Bergere on October 9.
1914	Writes a wildlife management guidebook.
1916	Develops a plan to protect the Gila Wilderness Area. This area becomes the first protected official wilderness region in a national forest.
1924	Begins a new job at the Forest Products Lab in Madison, Wisconsin.
1928	Works on a National Wildlife Survey, which aimed to develop ideas to conserve game animals, for The Sporting Arms and Ammunition Manufacturers' Institute.
1933	Begins teaching at the University of Wisconsin.

1934   Selected by President Franklin D. Roosevelt to serve on the President's Committee on Wildlife Restoration.

1935   Buys and restores land on the Wisconsin River.

1937   Begins work on a collection of nature stories called *Great Possessions*.

1948   Book is renamed *A Sand County Almanac* and is accepted by Oxford University Press. On April 21, Aldo dies of a heart attack while putting out a brushfire.

1949   *A Sand County Almanac* is published.

2001   A new edition of *A Sand County Almanac* is published by Oxford University Press. It includes new color photographs of The Shack and its surroundings.

FOR FURTHER INFORMATION

BOOKS

Anderson, Peter. *Aldo Leopold: American Ecologist*. Danbury, CT: Franklin
    Watts, 1995.
Patent, Dorothy Hinshaw. *Places of Refuge: Our National Wildlife Refuge
    System*. New York: Clarion Books, 1992.

WEB SITES

The Aldo Leopold Foundation
http://www.aldoleopold.org

The Aldo Leopold Nature Center
http://www.naturenet.com/alnc/

Ecology Hall of Fame
http://www.ecotopia.org/ehof/index.html

The Wilderness Society
http://www.wilderness.org/

LIST OF WORKS CONSULTED

ARTICLES

Bradley, Nina Leopold. "A Man for All Seasons." *National Wildlife* (April 14, 1998).

Raeburn, Paul. "A Passion for Nature as Great as Thoreau's." *BusinessWeek* (April 17, 2000).

BOOKS

Leopold, Aldo. *A Sand County Almanac*. New York: Oxford University Press, 1949.

Lorbiecki, Marybeth. *Aldo Leopold: A Fierce Green Fire*. New York: Oxford University Press, 1996.

———. *Of Things Natural, Wild, and Free: A Story About Aldo Leopold*. Minneapolis: Carolrhoda Books, 1993.

Meine, Curt. *Aldo Leopold: His Life and Work*. Madison, WI: The University of Wisconsin Press, 1988.

INDEX

ABOUT THE AUTHOR

Della Yannuzzi graduated from Kean College and is a teacher and writer. She enjoys working with preschool children and writing children's books. Della has published stories and articles in *Highlights for Children, Cobblestones, My Friend, New Moon,* and others. She has written biographies for young readers on Zora Neale Hurston, Wilma Mankiller, Mae Jemison, Ernest Hemingway, and Madam C.J. Walker. Her Hemingway biography was included in the 1999 New York Public Library's notable book list for teenagers. Della enjoys traveling, reading, and gardening in her spare time. She lives in Virginia with her husband, Michael, daughter, Cara, and lovable cat, J.D.